THE BEST OF

CHEFCLUB RECIPES TO SHARE

THE BEST OF

CHEFCLUB RECIPES TO SHARE

CHEFCLUB

PUBLISHING

2018, Snacking Media
53, rue de Chabrol
75010 Paris - France

All rights of translation, adaptation and reproduction, total or partial, for any use,
by any means whatsoever, reserved for all countries.

Legal deposit: June 2018
ISBN: 978-2-490129-04-1
Printed in Italy by Print Co in June 2018

SUMMARY

INTRODUCTION

When the ingredients of our cupboards become the big stars of small screens: phones, tablets, computers...Chefclub gourmet feasts are all over the world!

You are now part of more than 30 million suscribers all over the world who follow our recipe videos. We are very proud of our small team of 25 people from France, Italy, Brazil, Germany, the UK, and all over the world. Even if we satisfy our own cravings every day (as you can probably imagine!), we work hard and each of your comments or shares encourages us in our culinary adventures. So obviously, we wanted to first and foremost thank you from the bottom of our hearts for your commitment to us.

Chefclub desires to transform the kitchen into a space for sharing and emotions.

The videos, and now this first book, are there to guide, inspire, amuse, but above all share… the sections of the book are organised according to this idea.
The first part, *Family*, is dedicated to simple and delicious recipes that will have the whole family gathered round the table in the snap of your fingers!
The second part, *Friends*, includes snacks and appetizers, and the recipes are designed for sharing between friends.
The third part, *Love*, is slightly more elaborate, and requires careful attention…the same level of attention usually reserved for your other half.
As for the fourth part, the *Bonus* section is a gift! Have your cake and eat it!

Consume in moderation…

Happy reading and bon appétit!

The Chefclub team

45

RECIPES

TO

SHARE

It's reeeeeaaaaady!

FAMILY

VEGETABLE FLOWER TART

AN EDIBLE BOUQUET, PERFECT FOR A SUMMER'S DAY

 6 PEOPLE

 PREPARATION
50 minutes

 INGREDIENTS
1 shortcrust pastry sheet
1 green courgette
1 yellow courgette
1 carrot
1 aubergine
1 large mozzarella ball
2 eggs
150ml cream
1 tbsp mustard
Salt and pepper

 EQUIPMENT
1 large pie dish
1 peeler

1 Cut the courgettes, carrot, and the aubergine into thin and even long slices using a peeler.

2 Place the pastry in the bottom of the pie dish, spread the mustard over the pastry on the bottom of the dish, and then add the slices of mozzarella on top.

3 Roll the vegetable strips into tight rolls and place them end up in the pie dish. In a bowl, combine the eggs, cream, salt and pepper, and pour the mixture over the vegetable rolls.

4 Bake the vegetable flower tart for 35 minutes at 180°C. Serve warm with a salad on the side.

 CHEFCLUB TIP
This recipe is ideal if you have leftover vegetables lurking at the bottom of your fridge. To freshen wilted veggies, soak them in water with a little vinegar and two small spoonfuls of sugar to bring them back to life!

QUICK COTTAGE PIE

THE PERFECT MEAL FOR WHEN TIME IS SHORT
AND YOU'VE GOT HUNGRY MOUTHS TO FEED!

 6 PEOPLE

 PREPARATION
30 minutes

 INGREDIENTS
250g beef mince
1 can Heinz Baked Beans®
1 tsp Marmite®
75g tomato puree
1 onion
2 garlic cloves
100g frozen peas
400g potatoes
50g grated cheddar
Olive oil
Pepper

 EQUIPMENT
1 frying pan
1 oven-proof dish

1 In a frying pan, fry the chopped onions, beef mince and chopped garlic in a little olive oil for 5 minutes (1).

2 Whilst the mince is cooking, slice the peeled potatoes into very thin slices (2). To make the potato rose, lay a line of overlapping slices of potato, and then roll them up tightly from one end.

3 To the mince, add the tomato puree and Marmite®, then the Heinz Baked Beans® and frozen peas (3). Cook until the mixture is bubbling hot. Place the meat into an oven-proof dish and arrange a layer of potato on top. Add the rose to the middle of the pie.

4 Grate the cheddar and put it on top of the potato slices with a sprinkle of black pepper. Bake in the oven for 20 minutes at 200°C (4).

CHEFCLUB TIP
Heinz Baked beans® are an excellent source of fibre and protein, as well as counting as one of your 5-a-day. They lower cholesterol and reduce the risk of heart disease, making them perfect for a family-friendly meal. Use the low salt and sugar free versions for an even more nutritious meal!

FLAMBÉ PIZZA

MAMMA MIA, WE CAN SKIP THE PIZZERIA!

 4 PEOPLE

 PREPARATION
20 minutes

 INGREDIENTS
2 pizza dough
80g tomato sauce
1 mozzarella ball
4 slices of prosciutto ham
10 black olives
60ml rum
100g rocket
Oregano
Balsamic vinegar
Olive oil

 EQUIPMENT
4 straws

1 On the first rolled piece of pizza dough, spread the tomato sauce and add slices of the mozzarella and black olives, and sprinkle with a pinch of oregano (1).

2 Using a brush, paint water around the edge of the dough. Place the straws on the edge (2) and cover with the second piece of pizza dough. Fold the edges of the 2 doughs together tightly to make a seal (3-4). Blow into the straws to make the dough swell up (5), then remove the straws and quickly seal the edges of the dough together to maintain the air dome.

3 Bake for 12 minutes at 210°C. At the end of baking, pour the heated rum onto the pizza and light it with a match (6).

4 Use scissors to cut open the flamed pizza dome (7). Garnish the pizza with rocket leaves and prosciutto ham (8). Use the flamed dome as a salad bowl, filling it with rocket and seasoning with olive oil and balsamic vinegar (9).

 CHEFCLUB TIP
We all know that the best pizza has a crispy crust. To achieve a 'pizza oven' effect, you need spare roof tiles from your garage! Preheat your oven to the maximum temperature with the tiles inside, then cook your pizza on the tiles at the specified time and temperature. You'll see the difference!

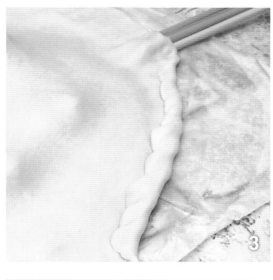

STUFFED PASTA CROWN

A FLOWER CROWN MADE OF PASTA! WILL IT BE ROMANCE OR ROYALTY IN THE KITCHEN TONIGHT?

 4 PEOPLE

 PREPARATION
40 minutes

 INGREDIENTS
400g shell shaped pasta
500g ricotta
200g ham
100g grated parmesan
100g grated mozzarella
300ml bechamel white sauce
½ bunch of parsley
Salt and pepper

 EQUIPMENT
1 large pie dish

1 Cook the pasta for 12 minutes in a large pot of salted boiling water until they are al dente.

2 Cut the ham into small pieces, and mix in a bowl with the ricotta, parmesan, chopped parsley, salt and pepper (1). Stuff the pasta shells with the mixture (2).

3 Spread the bechamel white sauce over the bottom of the pie dish, and arrange the pasta like flower petals on top (3). Sprinkle the grated mozzarella between the pasta shells (4).

4 Bake for 20 minutes at 190°C. Let it cool slightly before eating, and enjoy by picking out the pasta shells one by one.

 CHEFCLUB TIP
What's important here, is to not overcook the pasta, so it can be handled easily. To do this, once the cooking time is complete, drain the pasta and immerse immediately in water chilled with ice cubes! This will stop them from continuing to cook straight away.

JACKET POTATO BOATS

SAIL AWAY TO FOOD HEAVEN WITH THESE LOADED POTATO SKINS

 4 PEOPLE

 PREPARATION
40 minutes

 INGREDIENTS
4 large potatoes
100g diced bacon lardons
4 tbsp of crème fraîche
4 eggs
50g grated mozzarella
Parsley
Salt and pepper

 EQUIPMENT
1 baking tray
Baking paper

1 Cook the potatoes for 20 minutes in salted boiling water, then take them out and remove the middle of the potato with a spoon.

2 Fry the bacon in a pan, then spread a layer of the crème fraîche in the bottom of each potato skin, and add the cooked bacon on top. Crack an egg into each potato and sprinkle grated mozzarella on the egg white.

3 Bake for 15 minutes at 180°C. After baking, sprinkle with salt and pepper and a little chopped parsley before serving.

 CHEFCLUB TIP
To save time, you can cook the potatoes in the microwave! Prick them with a fork and microwave for about 10 minutes on full power.

MEDITERRANEAN PASTRY CROWN

BRING A TASTE OF ITALY TO YOUR TABLE WITH THIS SIMPLE PASTRY TART

 4 PEOPLE

 PREPARATION
30 minutes

 INGREDIENTS
1 tomato
1 courgette
1 puff pastry sheet
100g pesto
9 mini mozzarella balls
50g feta cheese
1 egg
5 black olives
Oregano

 EQUIPMENT
1 small bowl
1 baking tray

1 Unroll the puff pastry, place a bowl in the centre, and spread the pesto onto the pastry in a ring around the bowl.

2 Cut the tomatoes and courgettes into thick slices, and layer alternately on top of the pesto (1). Add the mini mozzarella balls and the feta onto the vegetables and top with a sprinkle of dried oregano.

3 Remove the bowl from the centre and cut a star in the middle of the pastry with a knife (2). Gently fold the outer edge of the pastry inwards and place the pastry star pieces over the top of the vegetables and cheese (3).

4 Brush the pastry with egg yolk and add slices of olives on top of the pastry star triangles. Bake for 20 minutes at 190°C and enjoy warm with salad on the side (4).

 CHEFCLUB TIP
If you don't have pesto at home don't worry, it is both easy and quick to make. Mix, in a blender, about 25g of fresh basil leaves with a pinch of salt, 8g of toasted pine nuts, 35g of grated parmesan, ½ a garlic clove and a drizzle of olive oil. You can add more or less olive oil to change the consistency of the pesto to suit your preference. Give it a go!

TOMATO & MOZZARELLA 3 WAYS

3 ALTERNATIVE WAYS TO ENJOY THIS CLASSIC COMBINATION

 6 PEOPLE

 PREPARATION
60 minutes

 INGREDIENTS
10 slices of bread
2 tomatoes
3 large mozzarella balls
50g green pesto
375ml white wine
200g small mozzarella balls
200g cherry tomatoes
1 garlic clove
Basil
Thyme
1 slice of prosciutto ham
2 eggs
100g flour
150g breadcrumbs
500ml vegetable oil
Olive oil
Salt and pepper

 EQUIPMENT
1 toaster
1 baking tray
Aluminium foil
Baking paper
Kebab skewers
1 saucepan

1 Sandwich:
On a square of aluminium foil (30x30cm) place a slightly smaller square of baking paper. Brush one side of a piece of bread with olive oil and place it on the paper, oil side down. Cover the other side of the bread with a layer of pesto, 2 slices of tomato, and 2 slices of mozzarella. Finish with a few extra blobs of pesto (1), then add a second slice of bread on top, and brush the top with more olive oil (2). Close the foil around the sandwich by wrapping up 3 sides, and cook for 4 minutes in a toaster (3).

2 Fondue:
Melt the small mozzarella balls in a saucepan with the white wine, and season with salt and pepper (4). Cut the bread into small crouton shapes, and brush them with a mix of the chopped garlic, thyme and olive oil. Bake for 5 minutes at 180°C (5). Make skewers of a cherry tomato, a basil leaf and the toasted crouton (6), then dip them in the fondue.

3 Croquette:
Cut the top off the large mozzarella balls to create a hat, leaving one edge still attached. Hollow out the middles and stuff them with chopped tomato, half a slice of prosciutto ham and a basil leaf (7). Coat the balls in flour, beaten egg, and breadcrumbs, and fry them for 4 minutes in hot oil. Enjoy all your creations (8-9)!

 CHEFCLUB TIP
Tips for selecting a good tomato; if it's soft and the stem falls away at first touch - be careful, this is too ripe...if it has a thin skin, it was grown in a greenhouse, and may not be as flavoursome.

QUICK QUICHE

SUPER EASY AND SPEEDY!

 4 PEOPLE

 PREPARATION
30 minutes

 INGREDIENTS
4 slices of bread
6 eggs
2 slices of ham
70g grated cheddar
70g grated mozzarella
1 red pepper
1 onion
1 bunch of chives
Salt and pepper

 EQUIPMENT
1 square baking tin
2 sheets baking paper

1 Place the sheets of baking paper across each other in the baking tin, and place the slices of bread with crusts removed (1) at the bottom of the tin.

2 Beat the eggs in a bowl and season with salt and pepper. Stir in the diced red pepper, chopped onion, chopped ham, chopped chives and both grated cheeses (2). Pour the mix into the baking tin (3).

3 Bake for 20 minutes at 180°C. After baking, cut the quiche into 8 triangles (4). Enjoy either hot at home or cold on the go. You choose!

 CHEFCLUB TIP
You can make this quiche even more light and fluffy by beating the egg whites first, then adding the beaten yolks and gently stirring in the rest of the mixture, before covering the slices of bread. You'll get XXL quiches with the same amount of ingredients!

BACON WRAPPED LASAGNE

A CRISPY WRAPPING FOR THIS DELICIOUS LASAGNE PRESENT

 6 PEOPLE

 PREPARATION
45 minutes

 INGREDIENTS
200g lasagne pasta sheets
250g beef mince
200g tomato sauce
500ml bechamel white sauce
30 rashers of bacon
200g grated mozzarella
1 onion
Mixed herbs

 EQUIPMENT
1 loaf tin
1 frying pan

1 Cook the mince and chopped onion in a frying pan, then add the tomato sauce and mixed herbs (1). Simmer for a few minutes, stirring regularly.

2 Fully cover the base and sides of the loaf tin with the bacon, placing them perpendicular to the walls of the loaf tin (2).

3 Place a layer of lasagne sheets on top of the bacon in the bottom of the tin (3). Add a layer of bechamel white sauce (4), a layer of grated mozzarella, and then a layer of the mince mix on top (5). Repeat the layers and finish with a layer of bechamel white sauce and grated mozzarella.

4 Fold the ends of the bacon rashers over the mozzarella to close the 'cake' (6-7) and bake for 45 minutes at 180°C (8). Once baked, turn it out the tin and enjoy hot (9).

 **CHEFCLUB TIP**
For a healthier option, you can replace the bacon with strips of different vegetables that have been sliced with a peeler: carrot, aubergine, courgette...the list continues...

1

2

3

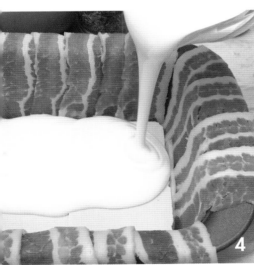

4

5

6

7

8

9

HOT DOG TART

A REVOLUTIONARY NEW WAY TO ENJOY A HOT DOG

 4 PEOPLE

 PREPARATION
30 minutes

 INGREDIENTS
2 sheets puff pastry
125g mozzarella
8 hot dog sausages
1 onion
1 egg yolk
200ml vegetable oil
Mustard
Ketchup

 EQUIPMENT
1 baking tray
Baking paper

1 Cut the mozzarella cheese into thin strips. Make a cut in the hot dogs down the length, and stuff the mozzarella strips into the gap.

2 Cut the pastry into a rectangle the same width as the full length of the hot dogs. Cut this rectangle into 5 strips, leaving the left side edge of the pastry uncut to hold it all together. Form a checkerboard of pastry and hot dog by alternating the hot dogs and strips of pastry, following the same process as the rainbow tart page 40.

3 Cut the onion into rings and fry for 3-4 minutes in hot oil. Cut the second puff pastry sheet to the same width as the checkerboard but make it slightly longer in length. Put the fried onion onto the second pastry sheet.

4 Put the checkerboard pastry sheet on top of the onion and fold the edges of the bottom sheet of pastry over to make the edges. Brush the pastry with egg yolk.

5 Bake for 15 minutes at 210°C, then decorate with mustard and ketchup and serve with some salad on the side.

 CHEFCLUB TIP
To make the original recipe for real fried onions, it's just as simple but requires a little more patience. Dip the onions in a mixture of milk, then salt, paprika and finally flour. Fry until golden brown.

CAULIFLOWER PIZZA

ANYONE WHO CLAIMS GLUTEN FREE IS TASTE FREE NEEDS TO TRY THIS!

4 PEOPLE

PREPARATION
35 minutes

INGREDIENTS
1 cauliflower
1 tsp cornflour
3 eggs
200g tomato sauce
3 slices of ham
1 large ball of mozzarella
12 black olives
Oregano
Basil
Parsley
Salt and pepper

EQUIPMENT
1 baking tray
Baking paper

1 Chop the cauliflower into very fine pieces, then add to it the eggs, salt, pepper, cornflour and chopped parsley, and mix well (1). On a baking tray lined with baking paper, make a disc with the cauliflower mix and bake in the oven for 10 minutes at 180°C.

2 Once cooked, add tomato sauce to your cauliflower pizza base (2). Top it with the oregano, ham, sliced mozzarella and black olives (3).

3 Bake in the oven for 15 minutes at 210°C. Garnish with fresh basil leaves and serve hot (4).

CHEFCLUB TIP
Cauliflower makes a great gluten free alternative to bread and pasta. You can make cauliflower rice or cous-cous by frying finely chopped cauliflower with a tablespoon of water for 5 minutes in a frying pan, or mixing with egg and cheese and frying for 5 minutes on each side to make an alternative slice of toast. It's low fat and low-carb too, so a great option for anyone watching their calorie intake!

EASY BEEF WELLINGTON

WE'VE TAKEN THE HASSLE OUT OF THIS CLASSIC DISH, BUT IT STILL LOOKS AND TASTES AMAZING

 4 PEOPLE

 PREPARATION
45 minutes

 INGREDIENTS
1 courgette
250g beef mince
100g grated parmesan
3 eggs
1 large mozzrella ball
2 shortcrust pastry sheets
1 egg yolk
Parsley
Salt

 EQUIPMENT
1 baking tray
1 grill pan
Baking paper

1 Cut the courgette into thin slices lengthways, then cook in a grill pan for 2 minutes on each side.

2 In a bowl, add the beef mince, grated parmesan, eggs, parsley and salt and mix together well (1). On a baking tray lined with baking paper, make a rectangle shape with the mince mix, then add a layer of grilled courgette on top, then a layer of sliced mozzarella (2-4).

3 Using the baking paper, roll the mince up into a sausage (5). Bake in the oven at 180°C for 15 minutes.

4 Unroll both sheets of pastry and make horizontal cuts 2cm wide across each sheet to give you strips of pastry. Peel alternative strips back in the opposite direction on one sheet, then add another strip from the second sheet perpendicular across the others, then fold the strips back over the top (6). Repeat this process to create a lattice.

5 Place the cooked mince sausage on the pastry lattice (7), then fold the pastry over the meat and brush the pastry with an egg yolk (8). Bake in the oven on a baking tray for 15 minutes at 180°C. Allow to cool a little and then enjoy (9).

CHEFCLUB TIP
You can change the flavours of this wellington easily. Simply replace the beef mince with any other meat to make your favourite flavour; for a lighter meal, try chicken or turkey mince instead of beef, or pork mince for a stronger flavour. You can also change the vegetable inside, instead of courgette - so many options, let your imagination run wild.

ZIPLOC® OMELETTE

THE NO-FUSS, EASY SOLUTION TO UNWANTED SCRAMBLED EGGS...

 2 PEOPLE

 PREPARATION
20 minutes

 INGREDIENTS
6 eggs
1 slice of ham
½ red pepper
½ green pepper
1 onion
100g grated mozzarella
100g grated cheddar
½ avocado
Tomato sauce
Salt and pepper

 EQUIPMENT
1 large saucepan
1 Ziploc bag®

1 Cut the peppers into small cubes, the ham into thin slices, and finely chop the onion and mix it all together.

2 Break the eggs into the Ziploc® bag and season with salt and pepper. Close the bag and shake vigorously! Open the bag and add the onion, peppers, ham and grated cheese (1). Close the bag and shake again to mix all the ingredients together.

3 Immerse the bag in the pan of simmering water (2), and cook for 15 minutes. Remove the omelette from the bag (3) and enjoy with tomato sauce and avocado on the side (4).

 CHEFCLUB TIP
In order to get an evenly cooked omelette, avoid putting the Ziploc® bag into direct contact with the pan. To do this, you can hold the bag in the water by piercing the top, and holding it with a pair of chopsticks resting on the edge of the pan - genius!

LITTLE BREAKFAST ROLL

WE VOTE BREAKFAST FOR EVERY MEAL OF THE DAY!

4 PEOPLE

PREPARATION
20 minutes

INGREDIENTS
4 bread rolls
100g diced bacon lardons
4 eggs
200ml crème fraîche
40g grated mozzarella
10g butter
Parsley
Salt and pepper

EQUIPMENT
1 baking tray
Baking paper

1 Cut the top off the bread rolls and remove the bread from the middle. Butter the bread roll lids, then cut them into soldiers.

2 Spread a layer of crème fraîche onto the bottom of the rolls, fry the bacon, then place it into the rolls as well. Add grated mozzarella on top of the bacon, and then break an egg into each roll.

3 Put the rolls and the bread sticks into the oven for 10 minutes at 180°C on a baking tray. Remove the rolls from the oven, season with salt and pepper and sprinkle with chopped parsley. Enjoy by dipping the toasted breadsticks into the cheesy and eggy bread roll centre.

CHEFCLUB TIP
To cook the bacon quickly, simply wrap it in paper towels and place in a microwaveable container for about 2 minutes. The bacon will be perfectly cooked, and the fat will be soaked into the paper towel instead of on the bacon.

RAINBOW TART

A BEAUTIFUL DISPLAY OF COLOUR THAT TASTES AS GOOD AS IT LOOKS

 4 PEOPLE

 PREPARATION
50 minutes

 INGREDIENTS
2 sheets of puff pastry
1 green pepper
1 yellow pepper
1 red pepper
1 orange pepper
1 large ball of mozzarella
4 slices of ham
1 egg
Salt and pepper

 EQUIPMENT
1 baking tray
Baking paper
Ruler
Pastry brush

1 **To prepare the base:**
Cut a square as large as possible in the first sheet of puff pastry, then brush the edges of the square with beaten egg (1). Place the slices of ham and pieces of mozzarella in the centre then sprinkle with salt and pepper (2).

2 **To prepare the checkerboard top:**
Cut another large square in the second sheet of puff pastry, and cut it all into 2cm wide strips. Position one strip vertically over the ends of the others on the left of the square (3). Fold the top strip back over the vertical strip of pastry, then do the same for every other strip (4). To finish, cut the peppers into strips about 1.5cm wide (5).

3 **To prepare the grid:**
Arrange strips of pepper of the same colour in a line alongside the vertical pastry strip, then cover over with the folded back strips of pastry (6). Fold the second set of pastry strips back to the left and place another line of pepper strips of another colour. Repeat the process alternating the peppers and strips to form a checkerboard (7). Arrange the remaining 3 strips of pastry on the outside frame to create a border around it.

4 Place the checkerboard sheet onto the base (8) and press lightly so the egg sticks the dough together. Brush the tart with beaten egg yolk. Bake for 30 minutes at 200°C and then enjoy hot (9).

 CHEFCLUB TIP
If you don't have a ruler handy to make the strips of pastry, use the cardboard packaging from the pastry to get straight edges. Take note, the more bands of pepper and pastry you do, the more impressive the result will be!

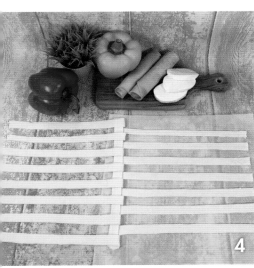

Nothing beats breaking bread with friends!

FRIENDS

CARBONARA CROWN

THE ULTIMATE CHEESY PASTA FONDUE FUSION

6 PEOPLE

PREPARATION
35 minutes

INGREDIENTS
250g spaghetti
1 camembert cheese
200g diced bacon lardons
100g grated parmesan
4 eggs
Cherry tomatoes
Basil

EQUIPMENT
1 round cake tin
1 saucepan

1 Cook the spaghetti for 8 minutes in a large saucepan of salted boiling water, and drain.

2 Fry the bacon in the saucepan. Add the cooked spaghetti, eggs and parmesan cheese. Mix everything together well (1).

3 Place the whole camembert (without its wooden box) in the centre of the round cake tin. Place the spaghetti mix all around the camembert (2).

4 Bake for 20 minutes at 210°C. After cooking, remove the top of the cheese (3) and garnish the crown with a few basil leaves and cherry tomatoes (4). Eat by dipping chunks of the pasta crown into the cheesy fondue.

CHEFCLUB TIP
To make the pasta even crispier, you can pan fry it. Pour the pasta mix into an oiled pan and cook without stirring. When it starts to stick together, use a lid to flip the pasta over and cook the other side for a few more minutes.

EASY CHEESY ONION RINGS

QUICK AND SIMPLE, BUT DELICIOUS EVERY TIME

 6 PEOPLE

 PREPARATION
15 minutes

 INGREDIENTS
4 red onions
1 block of mozzarella
150g flour
150g breadcrumbs
4 eggs
500ml vegetable oil
Tomato sauce

 EQUIPMENT
1 saucepan

1 Cut the onions into thick slices, then separate the rings with your fingers (1). Cut the mozzarella so you have long strips.

2 Take 2 onion rings of different sizes and fit pieces of the mozzarella between them (2). Repeat this process to make as many onion rings as possible then place them in the freezer for 1 hour.

3 Coat all the onion rings by dipping them into flour, then egg, and finally breadcrumbs (3). Fry for 5 minutes in hot oil. Serve hot and fresh with plenty of tomato sauce (4).

> **CHEFCLUB TIP**
> It's possible to replace the mozzarella with other cheeses, such as camembert. Just remember, try and use a cheese with the same texture as the mozzarella, so the onion rings are easy to assemble.

MEATBALL LOLLIPOPS

SNACK, STARTER OR A PICNIC MUST-HAVE?
THIS RECIPE IS YOUR GO-TO CROWD PLEASER

 3 PEOPLE

 PREPARATION
40 minutes

 INGREDIENTS
For 6 lollipops:
250g beef mince
6 mini mozzarella balls
6 small onions
12 rashers of bacon
1 egg
Barbecue sauce
Salt and pepper
Parsley

 EQUIPMENT
1 baking tray
6 kebab sticks
Baking paper

1 In a bowl, mix the mince, chopped parsley, egg, salt and pepper (1). Make a flat disc shape from the mix, then place a mini mozzarella ball in the middle, and close the mince around it to form a ball. Repeat until you have 6 meatballs.

2 Cut the ends off the onions, then remove the skin and carefully take off the outer layers, keeping them intact. Place the meatballs inside the onion rings (2) and wrap each one in 2 rashers of bacon.

3 Place a kebab stick in the centre of each ball (3), and bake for 30 minutes at 180°C on a baking tray. After baking dip the lollipops in barbecue sauce and serve (4).

 CHEFCLUB TIP
To avoid crying when cutting an onion, simply run it under the tap briefly before cutting. It's a little more tricky to cut a wet onion, but at least you'll be able to see what you're doing!

TRIPLE THREAT CHEESE FONDUE

THE FONDUE TO END ALL FONDUE'S....IT'S GOING DOWN IN THE HISTORY BOOKS!

 4 PEOPLE

 PREPARATION
35 minutes

 INGREDIENTS
1 large loaf of bread
3 x 125g of your favourite cheese for melting
50g diced bacon lardons
1 onion
1 tbsp grated parmesan
1 garlic clove
½ bunch of parsley
Dried rosemary
1 tbsp olive oil

 EQUIPMENT
1 baking tray
Baking paper

1 Cut 3 squares in the top of the loaf of bread, being careful not to cut through to the bottom. Cut the removed bread squares into breadsticks (1).

2 Fill each of the squares with a different type of your chosen cheeses (2-4). Add a topping to each cheese; for example fried onions, dried rosemary, and grilled bacon (5-6). Repeat the cheese and topping layers, and finish with a layer of cheese on the top of each square.

3 Combine the olive oil with finely chopped garlic, chopped parsley and parmesan cheese. Place the loaf of bread and the breadsticks on the baking tray, on top of baking paper, and brush the breadsticks with the olive oil mixture (7).

4 Bake for 30 minutes at 200°C (8). Serve hot by dipping the breadsticks into the melted cheese fondues (9).

 CHEFCLUB TIP
Contrary to what you might think, the softer and creamier cheeses don't necessarily contain more calories, in fact it's the opposite! Pressed and cooked hard cheeses contain very little water and therefore concentrate the fat. Hurrah for camembert!

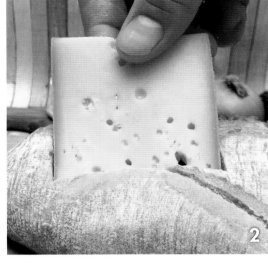

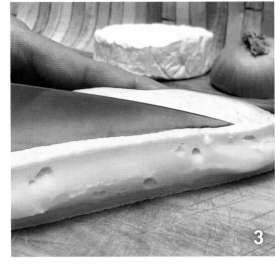

GIANT CURLY FRIES

YOU CAN MAKE THEM AS BIG AS YOU WANT!

 4 PEOPLE

 PREPARATION
35 minutes

 INGREDIENTS
300g potatoes
70g butter
1 tsp salt
1 tsp sugar
150ml water
80g flour
3 eggs
500ml vegetable oil

 EQUIPMENT
1 piping bag
1 piping nozzle
1 large saucepan

1 Peel and cook the potatoes in salted boiling water, then drain and mash them to get a smooth mixture (1).

2 In a saucepan, boil together the butter, sugar, salt and water. Remove the pan from the heat, and add the flour and mix well.

3 Beat the eggs together, and gradually add them to the dough mixture, mixing until the dough is smooth and thick (2).

4 Add the potato mash to the dough and place the whole mix in a piping bag. Pipe the mix in spirals straight into hot oil and cook until golden (3). Drain the fries on a paper towel and enjoy with tomato sauce (4).

CHEFCLUB TIP
For this recipe, the type of piping nozzle you use will make all the difference. A star nozzle will give a star shape with crispier edges, but if you have no piping set, simply use a freezer bag and cut a small corner off and pipe using that. Not as neat but still delicious!

FLOWER PETAL PIE

SHE LOVES ME...SHE LOVES ME NOT...BUT AT LEAST THERE'S PIE

 6 PEOPLE

 PREPARATION
60 minutes

 INGREDIENTS
3 sheets of puff pastry
300g beef mince
250g cheddar cheese
70g tomato puree
1 tbsp mustard
2 tbsp milk
Basil
Salt and pepper

 EQUIPMENT
1 large pie dish
1 cheese grater

1 Unroll the pastry, and using a glass, cut out as many circles of dough as possible and remove the excess dough.

2 Mix in a bowl with a fork the mince, tomato puree, mustard, chopped basil leaves, salt and pepper (1). Grate half the cheese. In the middle of half of the dough circles place a spoonful of the mince mixture, and in the other half put a spoonful of the grated cheese. Fold each circle in half, then bring the two points together to form petals (2).

3 Arrange the petals in the pie dish, alternating between meat and cheese rings, to form one large flower. Add a small cube of cheese to the hollows between the dough petals (3).

4 Brush the dough petals with a little milk, then bake for 45 minutes at 180°C. Enjoy! (4).

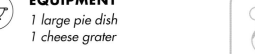

> **CHEFCLUB TIP**
> There are different methods to achieve a golden bake; use milk for just a light glaze, egg yolk will make it look bright and yellow, and olive oil will give a delicious taste. You can also use coffee grounds for sweet recipes!

MINI MOZZARELLA STICKS

SO GOOD YOU WON'T WANT TO SHARE....SHHHH

 2 PEOPLE

 PREPARATION
20 minutes

 INGREDIENTS
3 large balls of mozzarella
1 slice of prosciutto ham
1 sundried tomato
1 tsp ricotta
2 eggs
100g breadcrumbs
Basil
Vegetable oil
Ketchup

 EQUIPMENT
1 rolling pin
1 frying pan
1 baking tray

1 Grease an oven tray and place the 3 balls of mozzarella in the middle (1). Bake in the oven for 10 minutes at 180°C to melt the cheese. Remove the sheet of melted mozzarella, and using a rolling pin, roll into a rectangle shape.

2 Cut the mozzarella sheet in half, and add the prosciutto ham and sundried tomato to one end of one half, and ricotta and basil leaves to the end of the other half. Roll the mozzarella up to form 2 sausage shapes (2).

3 Cut 3cm pieces of the rolled mozzarella (3), and dip each piece in egg, and then breadcrumbs and fry for 3 minutes in a little oil till golden brown all over (4). Enjoy hot, dipped in ketchup.

 CHEFCLUB TIP
They are delicious plain but you can also stuff the mozzarella sticks with any fillings you want! Why not try creamy gorgonzola cheese, spicy jalepeños chillis or roasted red pepper in the middle? The possibilities are endless!

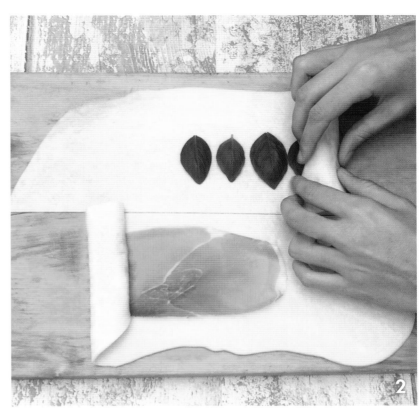

CHEESE FONDUE DIPPERS

ALL IN ONE EASY CHEESE FONDUE - READY TO SERVE AND ENJOY

 6 PEOPLE

 PREPARATION
25 minutes

 INGREDIENTS
2 puff pastry sheets
10 hot dog sausages
1 camembert cheese
100g sundried tomatoes
1 egg yolk
1 garlic clove
Chives

 EQUIPMENT
1 baking tray
Baking paper

1 Using a knife, cut a circle out of the top of the camembert and remove the rind lid. Add chopped sundried tomatoes (1), finely chopped garlic and chopped chives into the top of the camembert.

2 Put the rind lid back on the top of the camembert (2) and place it in the middle of a circular puff pastry sheet. Arrange 5 of the hot dog sausages around the camembert (3), and fold the pastry edges over the top of the hot dogs (4), then cut each hot dog into fifths (5).

3 Lift and rotate each hot dog piece about 90° (6). On the second sheet of puff pastry, cut pastry strips the size of the hot dogs and wrap them in the pastry, then cut them into fifths again.

4 Place the wrapped hot dogs in a layer on top of the previous ones to create a double layer around the camembert (7), then brush the pastry with egg yolk.

5 Bake for 20 minutes at 200°C on a baking tray. Once cooked, remove the lid from the camembert and dip the hot dogs into the fondue (8-9).

CHEFCLUB TIP

For this recipe, you can make it even more gourmet by adding a little white wine. Pour 50ml of wine inside the camembert with the sundried tomatoes, garlic and chives before cooking, then enjoy your amazing creation!

CANNELLONI BITES

A SPICY SURPRISE AWAITS INSIDE

2 PEOPLE

PREPARATION

40 minutes

INGREDIENTS

250g cannelloni pasta
2 garlic cloves
250g chopped tomatoes
5 drops of red Tabasco®
24 mini mozzarella balls
150g flour
4 eggs
100g breadcrumbs
Parsley

EQUIPMENT

1 Ziploc® freezer bag
1 baking tray
1 saucepan
Baking paper

1 Cook the cannelloni for 3 minutes in boiling salted water (1), then drain and cut each cannelloni in half.

2 In a frying pan cook the chopped tomatoes, finely chopped garlic, chopped parsley and 5 drops of Tabasco® for a few minutes (2). Place the sauce in a Ziploc® freezer bag.

3 On a plate, place the mini mozzarella balls and add a piece of cannelloni on top. Cut the corner off the bag and use it to fill the pasta tubes with the sauce, and close the tube by adding another mozzarella ball.

4 Dip the filled cannelloni in flour, then beaten egg, and finally breadcrumbs.Place them on a baking tray lined with baking paper (3), and bake for 15 minutes at 190°C. Enjoy hot (4).

CHEFCLUB TIP

You can choose what size you want for these, depending on the occasion! For smaller bite-size pieces you can use Rigatoni pasta tubes, or for larger ones you can use whole Cannellonni without cutting them in half. You can even add beef mince to the sauce if you like!

COURGETTE FRITTERS

READY TO EAT IN JUST 5 MINUTES

 4 PEOPLE

 PREPARATION
15 minutes

 INGREDIENTS
3 courgettes
3 large mozzarella balls
100g flour
3 eggs
50g breadcrumbs
50g grated parmesan
1L vegetable oil
Tomato sauce

 EQUIPMENT
1 peeler
1 frying pan
Toothpicks

1 Cut the courgette into thin slices using a peeler, and the mozzarella balls into thin slices with a knife.

2 Place 2 slices of courgette crossways over each other and put a slice of mozzarella in the middle (1). Fold the edges of the courgette around the mozzarella (2) and stick a toothpick into the centre of each parcel. Repeat the process to form as many courgette parcels as possible (3).

3 Coat the parcels in flour, beaten egg, grated parmesan and breadcrumbs. Fry the parcels for 2 minutes in hot oil, then drain and remove the toothpicks. Serve warm with tomato sauce to dip (4).

 CHEFCLUB TIP
Don't know when your oil is hot enough? Don't panic, just throw a small piece of courgette or stale bread in your oil and if the colour changes quickly, the oil is hot enough.

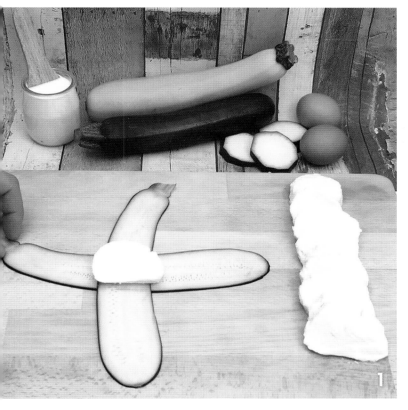

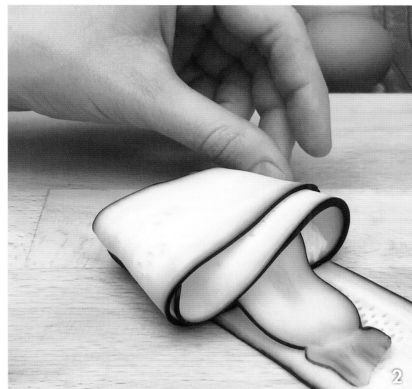

CRISPY OMELETTE

A SURPRISING ADDITION TO TAKE YOUR OMELETTE TO THE NEXT LEVEL

 6 PEOPLE

 PREPARATION
20 minutes

 INGREDIENTS
8 eggs
1 red pepper
1 green pepper
1 onion
1 large packet of crisps
Tomato sauce
Olive oil

 EQUIPMENT
1 large frying pan
1 ramekin

1 Beat the eggs in a bowl and stir in the crushed crisps. Chop the onion and peppers into small pieces and fry them in a pan for about 10 minutes. Then add the vegetables to the egg and crisps mixture (1).

2 Pour a drizzle of olive oil into a hot frying pan, and place an upturned ramekin dish in the centre of the pan (2). Pour the egg mixture around the ramekin and cook for 3 minutes. Turn the omelette over with a large plate and put it back on the heat for 3 minutes (3).

3 Slide the omelette onto a plate and pour tomato sauce into the ramekin. Serve hold or cold by dipping the omelette pieces into the tomato sauce (4).

 CHEFCLUB TIP
You can vary this recipe by choosing your favourite flavour of crisps to add...cheese and onion omelette anyone?

PIZZA BITES

SO YOU CAN GET YOUR PIZZA FIX WHENEVER YOU NEED IT

 4 PEOPLE

 PREPARATION
35 minutes

 INGREDIENTS
2 rolled pizza doughs
8 mini mozzarella balls
1 small piece of salmon
40g crème fraîche
2 slices of prosciutto ham
30g grated cheddar
50g feta
4 cherry tomatoes
Tomato sauce
Basil
Dill

 EQUIPMENT
1 ice cube tray
1 baking tray
Baking paper

1 Lay one rolled pizza dough over the ice cube tray (1) and using your fingers, gently push the dough into each of the wells.

2 Place in each row the following ingredients:
– ½ cherry tomato and a cube of feta cheese (2)
– 1 mini mozzarella ball and 1 basil leaf (3)
– 1 piece of prosciutto ham and grated cheddar cheese (4)
– 1 cube of salmon, crème fraîche and dill (5-6)

3 Cover the ice cube tray with the second piece of rolled pizza dough and use a rolling pin to seal the dough together. Remove the excess dough (7). Put the ice cube tray in the fridge for 10 minutes, then turn out the pizza cubes and separate them with a knife.

4 Arrange the pizza cubes on the baking tray lined with baking paper (8), and bake for 20 minutes at 180°C. Serve with tomato sauce (9).

CHEFCLUB TIP
This recipe is dedicated to anyone who loves a bite-sized snack! You can personalise the snack with your favourite pizza flavours or even just use the leftovers from your fridge!

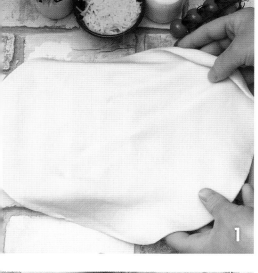

LASAGNE SANDWICH

LASAGNE TO GO!

 3 PEOPLE

 PREPARATION
15 minutes

 INGREDIENTS
For 3 lasagne toasties:
6 slices of white bread
50g butter
6 sheets of cooked lasagne
pasta sheets
1 carrot
1 onion
250g beef mince
100ml red wine
150g tomato sauce
300ml bechamel white sauce
200g grated mozzarella
Olive oil

 EQUIPMENT
1 toastie maker machine
1 frying pan

1 Spread the melted butter onto one side of each of the slices of bread, and then turn 3 pieces over and place a sheet of cooked lasagne pasta.

2 Brown the mince, carrot and onion in a frying pan with a little olive oil (1). Add the red wine and tomato sauce and mix together (2).

3 Add 1 tablespoon of the meat mix onto the lasagne sheet, cover with a second pasta sheet, and then add 1 tablespoon of bechamel white sauce. Finally cover with a third lasagne pasta sheet.

4 Sprinkle with grated mozzarella and close each sandwich with the remaining 3 slices of bread (3) with the buttered sides facing out.

5 Cook the lasagne sandwiches in the toastie machine for 3 minutes, and then serve with salad on the side (4).

 CHEFCLUB TIP
If you don't have a toastie machine you can still make these, just use a frying pan instead! Use a spatula to press down on the sandwich in the pan to get the nice crispy outside and flip carefully to make sure none of the filling falls out!

EGGS-PLODING BAGUETTE

PERFECT FOR YOUR WEEKEND BRUNCH

3 PEOPLE

PREPARATION
20 minutes

INGREDIENTS
1 baguette
10ml sunflower oil
6 eggs
150g diced bacon lardons
6 slices of edam
6 slices of cheddar
Chives

EQUIPMENT
Cling film
1 baking tray
1 frying pan
Baking paper

1 Cut the baguette into pieces 6cm in length (1). Form a hollow by pushing down on the inside of the bread.

2 Place clingfilm over a bowl. Brush the cling film with the sunflower oil and pour in an egg. Twist and knot the clingfilm to make a parcel. Repeat this 5 times. Cook the eggs in boiling water for 4 minutes, then add one into each piece of bread (2).

3 Cook the bacon in a frying pan, then add to the bread on top of the eggs. Add a slice of edam and a slice of cheddar on top of each (3).

4 Place under the grill for 5 minutes at 210°C. Sprinkle with chopped chives and serve (4).

CHEFCLUB TIP
Eggs are a complete source of protein, as they contain all nine essential amino acids we need and cannot produce in our body ourselves. They also contain selenium, vitamin D, B6, B12 and minerals such as zinc, iron and copper. A perfect way to fuel your body for the day!

ITALIAN HASSLEBACK CHICKEN

EASY, IMPRESSIVE AND FULL OF FLAVOUR

 3 PEOPLE

 PREPARATION
40 minutes

 INGREDIENTS
3 slices of bread
Olive oil
3 cloves of garlic
3 chicken breasts
20 cherry tomatoes
2 large mozzarella balls
100g spinach leaves
70g grated parmesan
Salt and pepper

 EQUIPMENT
Chopsticks
Baking tray
Baking paper

1 Cut the garlic into small pieces. Spread a little olive oil and some chopped garlic on the slices of bread (1).

2 Make incisions into the chicken breasts, using the chopsticks either side to make sure you don't cut through the breast entirely (2). Add thin slices of mozzarella (3) and chopped cherry tomatoes into the incisions (4). Season with salt and pepper and a drizzle of olive oil (5).

3 Add spinach leaves onto the slices of bread (6), and place a stuffed chicken breast onto each slice. Sprinkle grated parmesan over the top of each one (7), and place them on a baking tray lined with baking paper (8).

4 Bake the hassleback chicken in the oven at 190°C for 30 minutes. Enjoy hot (9) with salad on the side.

 CHEFCLUB TIP
The more cuts you make in the chicken the faster it will cook, just don't overload it with too many fillings! You can also vary this recipe by exchanging the tomatoes and spinach for chorizo and rocket or another of your favourite combinations.

For anyone who makes you swoon...

LOVE

PIZZA BOATS

YOU CAN SAIL ALL THE WAY TO FOOD HEAVEN...

 2 PEOPLE

 PREPARATION
30 minutes

 INGREDIENTS
1 pizza dough
250g beef mince
1 large mozzarella ball
12 sundried tomatoes
1 onion
2 cloves of garlic
100ml tomato sauce
1 egg
15g grated cheddar
Chives
Salt and pepper

 EQUIPMENT
1 baking tray
Baking paper

1 Cut the mozzarella and sundried tomatoes into pieces, and place them around the edges of the pizza dough. Fold the edge of the pizza dough over them, and form 2 points at either end.

2 Finely chop the onion and garlic and mix them with the mince, tomato sauce, salt and pepper and fill the middle of the dough with the mix. Sprinkle with the grated cheddar and break an egg in the middle.

3 Bake for 25 minutes at 180°C on a baking tray. Garnish with chopped chives and enjoy.

 CHEFCLUB TIP
If you want the egg to still have a runny yolk, add it to the pizza at the end of baking, letting it cook for just 5 minutes. Guaranteed success!

OMELETTE TOAST

OMELETTE AND TOAST COMBINED - IT'S GENIUS

 2 PEOPLE

 PREPARATION
15 minutes

 INGREDIENTS
4 slices of bread
1 red pepper
1 green pepper
2 slices of ham
4 eggs
80g grated mozzarella
Oil

 EQUIPMENT
1 frying pan
1 spatula

1 Using a knife, cut the middle out of the bread to leave you with just the crust (1). Cut the peppers and the ham into small pieces.

2 In frying pan, cook the peppers and ham in a little oil. Push ¼ of the mix together to form the shape of the bread crust, then place the crust over the top around the ham and pepper mix (2).

3 Beat an egg and pour it over the ham and peppers in the middle of the bread. Add the grated mozzarella on top and cook for 3 minutes (3).

4 Place the middle of the bread on the cheese, and using a spatula, flip the omelette over. Cook for 2 - 3 minutes on the other side. Repeat the process with the other 4 slices of bread and enjoy hot (4).

 CHEFCLUB TIP
You can use goats cheese instead of mozzarella for a stronger flavour which compliments the egg. Just ensure you cut the goats cheese into small pieces, so it cooks evenly.

CAULIFLOWER TOASTIE

...YOU CHOOSE YOUR FAVOURITE FILLING

2 PEOPLE

PREPARATION
20 minutes

INGREDIENTS
For 2 toasties:
1 small cauliflower
4 slices of ham
50g grated parmesan
150g grated cheddar
3 eggs
Chives
1 tsp paprika
Olive oil
Salt and pepper

EQUIPMENT
1 frying pan
1 blender
1 spatula

1 Put the cauliflower into a blender and mix with the eggs, grated parmesan, chives, paprika, salt and pepper.

2 Spread this mixture in a pan with a drizzle of olive oil, forming 4 squares with the spatula. Cook slowly over a very low heat for at least 5 minutes on each side, flipping them very carefully.

3 Add the ham and grated cheddar onto one slice, then close the toastie by putting one cauliflower slice on top of the cheese and ham on the other. Allow them to cook for a few minutes till the cheese is melted. Enjoy hot as a big toastie, or cut into triangles.

> **CHEFCLUB TIP**
> It's essential you cook the cauliflower on a low heat so it sticks together and doesn't dry out.

DORITOS® CHICKEN

CRISPY, CRUNCHY AND DEVISHLY TASTY

 2 PEOPLE

 PREPARATION
35 minutes

 INGREDIENTS
For 2 chicken breasts:
1 packet of Doritos® crisps
2 slices of cheddar cheese
2 chicken breasts
150g flour
2 eggs
Guacamole

 EQUIPMENT
1 baking tray
Baking paper

1 Crush the Doritos® crisps into small pieces (1), then pour the crushed crisps into a bowl.

2 Roll the cheese slices up tightly, then roll half a chicken breast around each piece of cheese (2).

3 Dip the chicken in flour first, then the egg and finally coat in the crushed Doritos® (3). Bake in the oven at 180°C for 25 minutes on a baking tray lined with baking paper, and serve hot with guacamole for dipping (4).

CHEFCLUB TIP
This is a great way to use up old crisps that have been left open and gone soft. In the oven they will crisp up again and give a nice crunchy coating. You can also swap the Doritos® flavour for your personal favourite!

THE SUSHI BURGER

A CULTURAL FUSION

 2 PEOPLE

 PREPARATION
30 minutes

 INGREDIENTS
For 2 sushi-burgers:
200g sushi rice
10g sugar
20ml rice wine vinegar
400ml water
4 prawns
1 fillet of salmon
1 avocado
½ cucumber
1 sheet of nori seaweed
Soy sauce
Salt

 EQUIPMENT
1 plastic bottle
1 small bowl
1 saucepan

1 Add to a saucepan the rice, sugar, vinegar, a pinch of salt and the water (1). Boil for 15 minutes until the rice is cooked.

2 Cut the salmon into small pieces, and slice the prawns in half lengthways. Then cut thin slices of avocado and cucumber (2).

3 Cut the top and bottoms off the plastic bottles to give you 2 plastic circle molds (3). Cut long strips from the seaweed sheet, 1.5cm wide (4).

4 Place 2 seaweed strips end to end and add the plastic circle mold over the top (5). Add the cooked rice to the inside to give the base of the burger, and then add a layer of chopped salmon, then avocado, then cucumber, then prawn (6).

5 Remove the plastic mold and use a small bowl to shape the top of the burger bun from the remaining cooked rice (7). Add the rice top then fold the seaweed strips over the top to hold it together (8). Serve with sesame seeds and soy sauce (9).

 CHEFCLUB TIP
The healthy omega-3 fats and selenium found in the salmon and avocado, and iodine in the nori seaweed, are all excellent nutrients for brain function. This makes this meal a 'smart' choice!

STUFFED GNOCCHI DONUTS

WE DONUT MIND WHICH FILLING YOU CHOOSE!

2 PEOPLE

PREPARATION
45 minutes

INGREDIENTS
For 4 donuts:
1kg potatoes
500g flour
8 rashers of bacon
1 large mozzarella ball
4 tbsp ricotta cheese
1 egg yolk
1 small glass of milk
8 cherry tomatoes
2 tsp baking powder
1 tbsp salt
Basil
500ml vegetable oil
Olive oil

EQUIPMENT
1 frying pan
1 rolling pin
Kitchen roll

1 Peel, cut and cook the potatoes in salted water and then drain. Mash them with the egg yolk, flour, milk, baking powder and salt, and mix until you get a smooth dough.

2 Place the dough on a floured surface (1) and roll it out with a rolling pin. Once rolled, cut 4 rectangles that are 20 x 8 cm.

3 Place 2 bacon rashers vertically on a chopping board, spaced slightly apart. Place the first dough rectangle horizontally across the bacon, and place into the middle of the dough the thin slices of cherry tomato and a layer of ricotta. Add a few basil leaves, sliced mozzarella and a drizzle of olive oil. Close the dough together and roll the bacon up around it, folding it together to form a ring (2). Repeat the process to form 4 donuts.

4 Fry the donuts in hot oil (3) until they have a nice golden colour. Drain them on some kitchen paper to remove any excess oil, then enjoy hot (4).

CHEFCLUB TIP
With any excess dough, make small round ball shapes and simmer them in boiling water. When they float to the surface you've got homemade gnocchi!

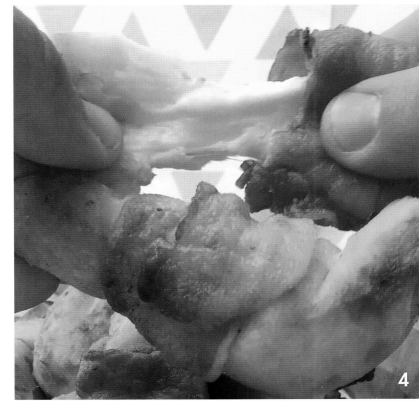

ONION ROSE TARTS

YOUR NEW FAVOURITE FLOWERS

2 PEOPLE

PREPARATION
35 minutes

INGREDIENTS
For 4 roses:
1 puff pastry sheet
1 large potato
½ camembert
4 rashers of bacon
2 red onions
40g onion jam
Olive oil
Pepper

EQUIPMENT
1 muffin tin

1 Cut the potatoes into thin slices about 3mm thick, and drizzle with olive oil and a sprinkle of pepper.

2 Cut the puff pastry into 4 horizontal rectangular pieces 8cm wide, and coat in the onion jam. Place a bacon rasher on the top half the pastry strip, then a layer of overlapping potato and thin slices of red onion. Add slices of camembert under the bacon, potato and onion on the pastry.

3 Fold the bottom half of the pastry and the camembert up over the top half, then roll the whole strip up from one end to make a rolled rose. Place each of the rolled roses in the muffin tin.

4 Bake for 20 minutes at 180°C. Allow the roses cool slightly before serving with courgette on the side.

CHEFCLUB TIP
You can try different cheeses and vegetables inside the rose instead of onion and camembert, to get a whole bouquet of edible flowers. Try courgette or aubergine with mozzarella or blue cheese for a change. The possibilities are endless!

UBER CREAMY SPAGHETTI

PERFECT FOR ENSURING EVERY SINGLE BITE IS TOTALLY CHEESE COVERED

 2 PEOPLE

 PREPARATION
30 minutes

 INGREDIENTS
1 Mont d'Or (or similar soft wooden-boxed cheese)
250g spaghetti
100g diced bacon lardons
50ml white wine
1 garlic clove
Parsley

 EQUIPMENT
1 saucepan
1 pair of tongs

1 Using a knife, cut a circle lid into the top of the cheese (1). Lift the lid of the cheese and add the white wine, cooked bacon, and finely chopped garlic onto the cheese (2).

2 Replace the lid on the cheese and bake in the oven for 20 minutes at 180°C. Cook the spaghetti in salted boiling water until al dente, and drain.

3 Lift the lid of the cheese and dip the pasta into it using a pair of tongs (3) to swirl the pasta round and completely coat it with the cheese. Serve the pasta garnished with chopped parsley (4).

 CHEFCLUB TIP
If you've forgotten a corkscrew don't panic! Remove the foil from the bottle head, hold the flame of a lighter to the glass just under the cork and as the air in the bottle warms, it will expand and the pressure will pop the cork out the top. Disaster averted!

LINGUINE IN A PARMESAN BOWL

NO NEED TO WASH UP, YOU CAN EAT THE BOWL!

 2 PEOPLE

 PREPARATION
30 minutes

 INGREDIENTS
For 2 bowls:
300g linguine pasta
200g grated parmesan
2 garlic cloves
30g pine nuts
Cherry tomatoes
Basil
Olive oil
Salt and pepper

 EQUIPMENT
2 bowls
1 baking tray
Baking paper

1 Spread grated parmesan in 2 circles on baking paper on a baking tray and bake in the oven for 15 minutes at 180°C. Remove from the oven and immediately place the soft parmesan disks on upturned bowls. As they cool they'll harden into a bowl shape.

2 Cook the linguine for 8 minutes in salted boiling water. Save a ladleful of the cooking water for later.

3 Fry the chopped garlic and pine nuts in a drizzle of olive oil. Add the cooked linguine, the ladle of cooking water, some fresh basil leaves and the grated parmesan, and then mix it all together.

4 Fill the parmesan bowls with the linguine and garnish with the cherry tomatoes, salt and pepper. Enjoy!

 CHEFCLUB TIP
You can also make the parmesan bowls in the microwave; place the grated parmesan circle on baking paper and cook for 45 seconds on full power!

THE SUSHI BALL

WITH A HEART OF GOLD

 2 PEOPLE

 PREPARATION
40 minutes

 INGREDIENTS
For 2 sushi balls:
200g sushi rice
4 rashers of bacon
1 avocado
2 eggs
Pepper

 EQUIPMENT
2 bowls
1 baking tray
Baking paper
4 pieces of clingfilm

1 Grill the bacon in the oven for 15 minutes at 170°C (1). Cook the sushi rice for 12 minutes in boiling water, and boil the eggs for 4 minutes.

2 Form 2 circles out of the rice on clingflim sheets (2). Peel, pit and thinly slice the avocado (3), and arrange the slices in a rosette on the rice (4).

3 Place a second sheet of clingfilm over the avocado, then turn it over and place inside a bowl (5). Remove the top sheet of cling film.

4 Sprinkle the chopped bacon over the rice and place the peeled eggs in the middle with a twist of pepper (6). Close the clingfilm around the ball and twist to form 2 tight balls (7-8) before removing the clingfilm. Serve fresh straight away (9).

 CHEFCLUB TIP
For this recipe, rinse the sushi rice in cold water before cooking. This gets rid of some of the starch and ensures it's still sticky enough after cooking, ready to form perfect rice balls!

ITALIAN CROQUE-MONSIEUR

AN ODE TO OUR ITALIAN FRIENDS IN THE FORM OF A TOASTIE

2 PEOPLE

PREPARATION
30 minutes

INGREDIENTS
For 2 toasties:
4 slices of bread
4 slices of prosciutto ham
2 large balls of mozzarella
200ml cream
100g grated parmesan
3 eggs
300ml semi-skimmed milk
100g flour
Basil
Olive oil
Salt and pepper

EQUIPMENT
Clingfilm
1 oven dish
1 frying pan

1 Spread olive oil on each slice of bread, cut the mozzarella into slices and place 2 mozzarella slices, 2 prosciutto ham slices and 1 basil leaf on 2 of the slices of oiled bread. Add salt and pepper and close the sandwiches with the remaining bread slices.

2 Dip the sandwich in milk, flour and then beaten eggs, then fry in a pan for a few minutes on each side over a medium heat.

3 Cut 2 pieces of clingfilm and place a sandwich on each piece, then close the clingfilm and twist to form 2 balls. Let that chill for 10 minutes in the fridge. Meanwhile, make a cheese sauce by heating cream and grated parmesan over a low heat.

4 Take the sandwich balls out the fridge, remove the clingfilm, place them in an oven dish and bake for 15 minutes at 180°C. Serve the croque-monsieurs straight from the oven with the parmesan cream sauce. Enjoy!

CHEFCLUB TIP
If you're fed up with eggs for everything these days, switch them for honey instead. For example, mix a tablespoon of lavender honey with milk and you'll get a sweet and savoury mix instead. Trust us here, it's delicious!

AVOCADO SURPRISE

EVERYTHING YOU NEED FOR THE PERFECT BREAKFAST, ALL WRAPPED UP IN ONE

 2 PEOPLE

 PREPARATION
25 minutes

 INGREDIENTS
For 2 avocado parcels:
2 avocados
6 rashers of bacon
2 eggs
50ml vegetable oil
Salt and pepper

 EQUIPMENT
Clingfilm
2 ramekins
1 saucepan

1 Place a square of clingfilm over each ramekin then brush the inside with a little oil. Crack an egg into each ramekin and close the clingfilm around the egg, cooking the parcel for 4 minutes in boiling water (1).

2 Cut the avocados in half and remove the skin, the stone, and a little of the flesh in the middle to make room for the egg.

3 Remove the clingfilm from the eggs and gently place them in the centre of the avocados (2). Place the other half of each of the avocados on top and wrap the whole avocado in 3 rashers of bacon (3).

4 Fry the avocados in a pan for 10-12 minutes, turning frequently to cook all the bacon. Serve hot (4).

CHEFCLUB TIP
You can also bake the bacon wrapped avocaodos instead of frying them. Bake for around 15 minutes at 160°C and the result will be just as beautiful as if you'd fried them!

ULTIMATE MASHED POTATO NESTS

OOZING WITH CHEESE, BACON AND HAPPINESS

 2 PEOPLE

 PREPARATION
50 minutes

 INGREDIENTS
For 4 nests:
500g potatoes
125g diced bacon lardons
1 camembert
1 egg
50g butter
50g grated parmesan
Parsley
Salt and pepper

 EQUIPMENT
1 piping bag
1 piping nozzle
1 baking tray
1 frying pan
Baking paper

1 Peel and cook the potatoes in boiling salted water, then mash the potatoes with egg, parsley, grated parmesan, butter, salt and pepper, and mix well to achieve a smooth mash.

2 Fry the bacon in a pan until it is crispy, and then cut the camembert into small chunks.

3 Place the mashed potato in the piping bag and pipe small nests onto baking paper on a baking tray. Fill the nests with the bacon and the camembert chunks.

4 Bake the nests for about 15 minutes at 180°C to get a crisp coating and melted cheesy middle. Enjoy hot and fresh.

 CHEFCLUB TIP
No piping bag? No problem! Use a freezer bag instead by simply cutting off one of the corners!

FLOWER TARTS

EVERYONE WANTS TO TUCK INTO THIS BEAUTIFUL BUNCH

 2 PEOPLE

 PREPARATION
15 minutes

 INGREDIENTS
1 pizza dough
4 hot dog sausages
4 eggs
80g grated mozzarella
Chives
Salt and pepper

 EQUIPMENT
4 kebab skewers
1 ramekin
1 toothpick
1 baking tray
Baking paper

1 Poke the kebab skewer through the hot dogs (1), remove the end pieces and cut slices into them without cutting all the way through. Take the skewers out and bend the hotdogs into circles.

2 Cut 4 circles out of the dough using a ramekin, and place a hotdog on each. Use a toothpick to fold the dough between the hot dog slices to make small flowers (2).

3 Add grated mozzarella to the middle of the flowers and season with salt and pepper. Bake for 10 minutes at 180°C on a baking tray.

4 Place an egg yolk in the middle of the flower and bake again for 3 minutes at 180°C (3). Garnish with chopped chives and enjoy with salad on the side (4).

 CHEFCLUB TIP
You can change the flavour of the middle of the flowers easily; simply substitute the egg yolk for a mini-mozzarella ball, for a creamy white centre.

THE MAGIC SALAD

YOU CAN EVEN EAT THE BOWL YOU SERVE IT IN

2 PEOPLE

PREPARATION
15 minutes

INGREDIENTS
For 2 salads:
2 sheets of rice paper
16 prawns
200g rice noodles
1 carrot
½ cucumber
½ lime
2 tbsp soy sauce
Sesame seeds
Peanuts
Fresh coriander
200ml vegetable oil
Salt and pepper

EQUIPMENT
1 large saucepan

1 Heat the vegetable oil in the saucepan and fry the rice paper sheets one at a time to allow them to puff up.

2 Fry the prawns and sesame seeds in a frying pan in a little vegetable oil. Meanwhile leave the rice noodles to soak in boiling water, and cut the carrot and cucumber into thin batons.

3 Prepare the dressing by mixing the lime juice with the soy sauce and 1 tablespoon of vegetable oil.

4 Prepare the salad in the fried rice paper with the noodles, carrots, cucumber and prawns, and cover in the dressing. Add some fresh coriander leaves, peanuts, salt and pepper, and enjoy.

CHEFCLUB TIP
This recipe also works as a spring roll. Soak the rice paper in hot water for a few seconds, then put it on a damp cloth and leave it to soften. Divide the ingredients and roll them tightly to form spring rolls, then enjoy!

One last bite for the road...

BONUS

CHURRO ICE CREAM BOWLS

DOES LIFE GET ANY BETTER THAN THIS COMBINATION?

 3 PEOPLE

 PREPARATION
25 minutes

 INGREDIENTS
For 6 churro bowls:
60g butter
70g sugar
250ml water
225g flour
2 eggs
500ml vegetable oil
Cinnamon
Chocolate sauce
6 scoops of vanilla ice-cream

 EQUIPMENT
1 muffin tin
1 piping bag
1 star piping nozzle
1 saucepan

1 In a saucepan, over low heat, mix the butter, 30g sugar and the water, and then bring to a boil. Add the flour, then lower the heat and mix (1).

2 Let the dough cool, then add the eggs and mix the dough well. Put the dough in a piping bag.

3 Use an upside down muffin tin to pipe the dough over the muffin tin compartments (2). Place the tin in the freezer for 40 minutes until the dough is frozen together and can be removed from the tin intact (3).

4 Fry the dough in boiling oil for a few minutes until golden brown. Drain any excess oil on kitchen paper, and roll the churro bowl in a mix of cinnamon and sugar.

5 Pour chocolate sauce into the churro bowl and add a ball of vanilla ice-cream. Drizzle more chocolate sauce on top and serve straight away (4).

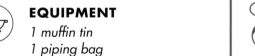

> **CHEFCLUB TIP**
> You can use this trick to make savoury versions too. Replace the churro dough with mashed potato instead and use it as a bowl to hold gravy or your favourite sauce, perfect for sausage and mash!

THE BROOKIE

FOR WHEN YOU JUST CAN'T CHOOSE BETWEEN A BROWNIE OR A COOKIE...

6 PEOPLE

PREPARATION
60 minutes

INGREDIENTS
315g flour
200g sugar
150g brown sugar
190g butter
3 eggs
120g dark chocolate
50g chocolate chips
1L vanilla ice-cream
80g pecan nuts
Caramel sauce

EQUIPMENT
1 square baking tin
1 whisk

1 **Cookie dough:**
Whisk the brown sugar and one egg together until the mixture lightens in colour (1). Add 100g of melted butter, 225g of sieved flour and the chocolate chips (2), and mix well to achieve a smooth dough. Leave to chill in the fridege for 15 minutes.

2 **Brownie dough base:**
Melt dark chocolate and 90g of butter (3) in a bowl over hot water. Stir in 2 eggs and add 90g of sieved flour, the sugar, and the chopped pecans (4). Mix until smooth.

3 Grease the tin and pour in the brownie batter. Remove the cookie dough from the fridge and crumble it onto the top of the brownie dough (5-6). Bake for 30 minutes at 180°C, then allow the cake to cool.

4 Remove the vanilla ice-cream from the tub and use the tub as a cutter to cut into the cake (7). Put some of the ice-cream back in the box and spread it over the brookie (8). Enjoy with caramel sauce in your bowl (9)!

CHEFCLUB TIP
If you prepare the brownie and cookie doughs in advance, you'll get an even better result! Store the 2 doughs in the fridge overnight to get a big cake which is crispy on the outside and soft and fluffy on the inside!

THE PEAR PARCEL

IMPRESS YOUR FRIENDS WITH THIS BEAUTIFUL CREATION

 2 PEOPLE

 PREPARATION
45 minutes

 INGREDIENTS
For 2 pears:
1 puff pastry sheet
2 pears
300g sugar
100g chocolate
300ml water
10 walnuts
25g caramel sauce
1 vanilla pod
1 egg yolk
1 cinnamon stick

 EQUIPMENT
1 apple corer
1 baking tray
Baking paper
1 saucepan

1 Slice the vanilla pod in half, and use a knife to scrape the seeds out. Pour the sugar, water, cinnamon and vanilla (seeds and the pod) into a saucepan and bring to the boil.

2 Immerse the peeled pears in the syrup for 10 minutes. Remove from the heat and allow to cool. Cut and keep the top of the pears, and remove the stem and the cores with the apple corer.

3 Place the pears upright on baking paper on a baking tray. Mix the nuts with the caramel sauce and fill the inside of the pears with the mix. Then put the pear tops back on top. Unroll the pastry sheet, cut it into 2cm strips, and wrap the strips around the pear. Brush the pastry with egg yolk.

4 Bake for 30 minutes at 170°C. Serve the pears on caramel sauce, then pour melted chocolate over the pears and decorate with a few chopped walnuts. Enjoy!

 CHEFCLUB TIP
If you want to impress your guests and really make your pears shine, brush the pastry with a mix of 3 teaspoons of icing sugar and 3 teaspoons of water as soon as you take it out the oven.

NUTELLA ® AND BANANA CROWN

THIS REALLY IS PUDDING ROYALTY!

 4 PEOPLE

 PREPARATION
15 minutes

 INGREDIENTS
1 sheet of puff pastry
1 banana
6 tbsp Nutella®
100g milk chocolate
1 egg yolk

 EQUIPMENT
1 ramekin
1 pastry brush

1 Peel and slice the banana into pieces about 1.5cm long, and arrange them on top of the puff pastry, spaced slightly apart. Pour Nutella® onto the banana slices (1).

2 Cut strips lengthways (about 2cm wide) on the remaining pastry (2), then roll up the dough on itself. Join the 2 ends of the dough together to form a crown (3).

3 Brush the pastry with the egg yolk. Place a ramekin in the center of the crown, and fill it with squares of milk chocolate.

4 Bake the crown for 30 minutes at 180°C (4). Enjoy by dipping pieces of crown into the melted chocolate.

> **CHEFCLUB TIP**
> Don't throw away the banana peel, make a cake! Separate an egg into white and yolk, then whisk the egg white. Wash the banana peel with water and chop it into small pieces. In a bowl, mix the egg yolk with 20g of butter, 3 tablespoons of sugar, 1 small cup of flour, 1 teaspoon of baking powder and the banana peel, then fold in the egg white. Bake for 20 minutes at 180°C and you'll get an unbeatable mini-cake, perfect for snacking!

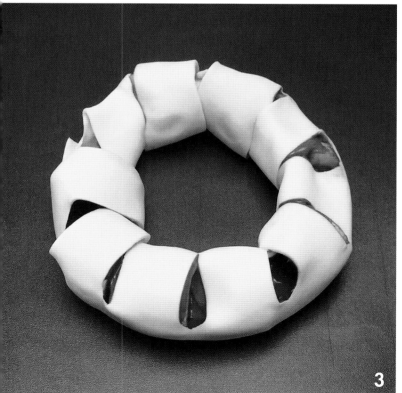

GIANT STUFFED COOKIE

IT'S IMPOSSIBLE TO RESIST THE MELTING CHOCOLATE MIDDLE...

 6 PEOPLE

 PREPARATION
40 minutes

 INGREDIENTS
200g butter
200g brown sugar
350g flour
3 eggs
300g chocolate chips
250g Kinder® Maxi bars

 EQUIPMENT
1 round cake tin
1 baking tray
Baking paper

1 Mix the softened butter, flour, brown sugar, eggs and chocolate chips together in a bowl (1).

2 On a lined baking tray, form a disc with half the cookie dough and place in the fridge for 30 minutes.

3 Grease the cake tin and spread the other half of the cookie dough inside the bottom and sides of the tin (2). Then place the Kinder® chocolate bars in circles inside.

4 After chilling, use a plate to cut an exact circle of dough the same size as the tin from the chilled cookie disc. Remove the excess dough.

5 Place the disc of cookie dough on top of the Kinder® chocolate (3) and bake for 25 minutes at 180°C. Remove the tin and enjoy warm (4).

 CHEFCLUB TIP
To help with cutting and lifting the cookie dough, it must be allowed to chill in the fridge. If you feel it's too soft or may break, put it in the freezer for a few minutes then try again!

ISLAND FISHBOWL

BRINGING YOUR VERY OWN TROPICAL ISLAND TO LIFE

 8 PEOPLE

 PREPARATION
20 minutes

 INGREDIENTS
120g vanilla ice-cream
1 packet of crocodile sweets
1 packet of green Nerds®
700ml of Malibu®
200ml of Blue Curaçao
1L of Sprite®
1 lime
2 lemons
20 ice cubes
2 cherries

 EQUIPMENT
1 glass fishbowl
1 tall glass
Straws

1 Mix 8 ice cubes with 100ml of Malibu® and the vanilla ice-cream together in a blender (1). Pour the mixture into a tall glass and place it in the middle of the fishbowl (2).

2 Fill the fishbowl with the rest of the ice cubes and the crocodile sweets (3). Pour in 600ml of Malibu®, the blue Curaçao, and the Sprite® (4), then add some green Nerds® (5).

3 Cut some slices of lemon, and arrange them around the edges of the bowl (6).

4 Cut the lime into 2, then make 4 cuts towards the base of the lime end and push down, placing it on top of a straw with 2 cherries, to create a palm tree and coconuts (7-8). Plant your palm tree on the 'island' and arrange more straws in the 'water' (9). Cheers!

 CHEFCLUB TIP
To make an even crazier cocktail, add fish and shell sweets and your aquarium will really come to life! You can also use transparent straws to enjoy the beautiful blue sea colour all the way to your mouth!

HONEY AND LEMON COCKTAIL

THIS HONEY AND LEMON TONIC INCLUDES A SURPRISING EXTRA KICK!

 3 PEOPLE

 PREPARATION
20 minutes

 INGREDIENTS
For 3 lemons:
3 lemons
200ml prosecco
200ml vodka
120g honey
Mint leaves

 EQUIPMENT
1 hand blender
1 jug
1 ice cube tray
1 fine strainer
1 glass

1 Cut the top off the lemons and remove the pulp from inside. Place the pulp in a strainer and squeeze all the juice out using the bottom of a glass. Save the empty lemons for serving.

2 Spread the lemon juice evenly between the wells in the ice cube tray, filling them ⅔ full. Add vodka, a few drops of honey and a mint leaf into each compartment to fill the tray completely.

3 Place the ice cube tray in the freezer for 1 hour to form the lemon ice cubes. Place the whole lemons in the freezer as well.

4 Remove the ice cubes from the freezer and place them in a jug. Pour the prosecco into the jug and mix everything together to create a slushy. Pour the lemon vodka slush back into the whole lemons to serve. Cheers!

 CHEFCLUB TIP
If, like most people, you forget to make ice cubes in advance and find yourself without them when you need them most, here's a tip that will save you time: use boiling instead of cold water in your ice cube tray, your ice will form a lot faster!

WHISKEY AND COKE SLUSHY

THE PERFECT DRINK ON A HOT SUMMERS DAY (OR NIGHT!)

 6 PEOPLE

 PREPARATION
30 minutes

 INGREDIENTS
1.5L of Coca-Cola®
700ml whiskey
1 lime
2 cherries
2 strawberries

 EQUIPMENT
1 blender
1 ice cube tray

1 Pour the Coca-Cola® into the ice cube tray, and place it in the freezer for 3 hours (1).

2 Remove the frozen Coca-Cola® cubes from the freezer, and put them in a blender with the whiskey. Blend together (2).

3 Pour the slushy mix into glasses and decorate with slices of lime, cherries and strawberries (3-4). Cheers!

 CHEFCLUB TIP
To make this without a blender, mix the juice of a lemon with the Coca-Cola® and place in an airtight container in the freezer until the liquid is completely frozen. To serve, take it out and scrape the surface with a fork. Divide the scrapings between glasses and add the whiskey before serving!

INDEX

THANK YOU AND MERCI!

We are a small team of 25 people in Paris, independent of any corporation, and your trust in us has allowed us to carefully curate this book with the same passion that we pour into our work everyday for Chefclub videos.

We chose Paris, the culinary capital of the world, to settle down. We are very proud of the culinary diversity that our team brings; English, French, Japanese, Brazilian, Argentinian, Italian and Chinese foodies all come together.
We seek to explore cuisines from around the world and learn from each others' experiences and differences.
Each country brings its passion and traditions and the UK is no exception, it has served as an inspiration for several of the recipes you'll find in this book, and no longer will we be known globally as a nation full of bad food!

We hope you will have as much pleasure discovering this book as we have had making it.

The Chefclub team